The Barnyard Bunch

GOOFY GOATS

Ryan James

Norwood House Press

Cataloging-in-Publication Data

Names: James, Ryan.
Title: Goofy goats / Ryan James.
Description: Buffalo, NY : Norwood House Press, 2026. | Series: The barnyard bunch | Includes glossary and index.
Identifiers: ISBN 9781978574298 (pbk.) | ISBN 9781978574304 (library bound) | ISBN 9781978574311 (ebook)
Subjects: LCSH: Goats--Juvenile literature. | Livestock--Juvenile literature.
Classification: LCC SF383.35 J359 2026 | DDC 636.3'9--dc23

Published in 2026 by
Norwood House Press
2544 Clinton Street
Buffalo, NY 14224

Designer: Rhea Magaro
Editor: Kim Thompson

Photo credits: Cover, p. 1 Narong Khueankaew/Shutterstock.com; p. 5 Vjacheslav Shishlov/Shutterstock.com; p. 6 yevgeniy11/Shutterstock.com; p. 7 Reddogs/Shutterstock.com; p. 9 Lelechka/Shutterstock.com; p. 10 Tom Meaker/Shutterstock.com; p. 11 Nik Hisham/Shutterstock.com; p. 12, 13 ollirg/Shutterstock.com; p. 14 Annabell Gsoedl/Shutterstock.com; p. 15 Kikujiarm/Shutterstock.com; p. 17 winnievinzence/Shutterstock.com; p. 18 Nataliia Melnychuk/Shutterstock.com; pp. 19, 21 Rita_Kochmarjova/Shutterstock.com;

Printed in the United States of America

CPSIA compliance information: Batch #CSNHP26: For further information contact Norwood House Press at 1-800-237-9932.

TABLE OF CONTENTS

GOOFY GOATS

Goats are farm animals.

They live in the barnyard.

HOW GOATS LOOK

A goat has two **horns** on the top of its head.

Goats have **beards**. They have **wattles** on their necks.

Goats have short hair. Their hair comes in many colors. It has different patterns.

HOW GOATS SOUND

A goat makes a noise that sounds like "baa" or "maa."

This is called **bleating**. Goats **communicate** by bleating.

Adult male goats have deep bleats. They use their bleats to attract females.

WHAT GOATS EAT

Goats are **herbivores**. They eat only plants. When it is warm outside, goats like to eat grass.

They **graze** in **pastures**. They try to find the healthiest grass to munch.

When it is cold outside, goats stay in the barn. They eat **hay**.

HOW GOATS GROW UP

Baby goats are called kids.

Kids like to run around and jump on things.

FUN ON THE FARM

Goats are **curious**. They like to learn about new people and new things.

GLOSSARY

beards (beerdz): tufts of hair that grow under a goat's chin

bleating (BLEE-ting): making a cry that sounds like "baa" or "maa"

communicate (kuh-MYOO-ni-kate): to share information and feelings

curious (KYOOR-ee-uhs): excited to know or learn about something

graze (graze): to feed on grass that is growing in a field

hay (hay): long grass that is cut, dried, and used as food for farm animals

herbivores (HUR-buh-vorz): animals that eat only plants

horns (hornz): hard, pointy parts on the top of a goat's head

pastures (PAS-churz): grassy fields where animals graze

wattles (WAH-tuhlz): little pieces of skin that hang from a goat's neck

THINKING QUESTIONS

1. What are baby goats called?
2. What sounds do goats make?
3. What do goats like to eat?
4. How do goats communicate with each other?
5. Why are goats known as curious animals?

INDEX

ABOUT THE AUTHOR

Ryan James lives in the mountains of North Carolina, where he goes hiking with his dog Bailey. He loves fly fishing, visiting farms in the area, and picking fresh produce. He has always enjoyed writing and wrote his first book as a teenager.